Copyright © 2021 Tekkan
Artwork Copyright © 2021

All rights reserved.
First Printing, 2021
ISBN 978-1-7363537-2-1

To contact Tekkan please email:
buddhaboy1289@gmail.com

How to Read My Poems

I want to be direct in my meaning — I want people to clearly understand my meaning. My wordiness is inspired by Shakespeare, and the (aimed-for) concision is in imitation of Japanese style. Using the sonnet with the tanka, I mix the sensibility of the Occident and the Orient — which I have done by living in England, Japan, and America.

I have married the sonnet to the tanka. Often, I don't rhyme my sonnets, because I want freer expression. I tell a story in the sonnet — using three quatrains separated by line spaces, and a final couplet. The story builds to a conclusion in the couplet. The tanka is a commentary, or a counterpoint, to the sonnet — the combined poems have two endings.

Recently I have added limericks, doggerel, and rhymed sonnets into my repertoire. The limericks have a rhyme scheme but the tanka do not.

I don't punctuate much in my poetry. I want the words themselves to do the work. There is logic between words, and the forms provide structure. By not using punctuation I hope to direct readers to carefully attend to each word — to appreciate the graininess of words.

Reading my poems silently and reading them aloud may be different experiences. The way I've written, there's not always a pause intended at the end of the line.

Hint: *My poems are to be recited not as lines but as phrases, and a phrase often overflows the break at the end of a line. I pause and take a breath where it seems natural for me to pause. Another person may pause differently than I do.*

Each poem is a piece of a mosaic, and it is my hope that the collection of poems forms an accurate portrait of consciousness.

My daughter, *Jocelyn MacDonald*, is a wonderful artist. Her artwork graces this book.

I am Barry MacDonald. I received the *dharma* name *Tekkan*, which means "Iron Man," a settled practitioner of great determination.

— *Tekkan*

Everyday Mind XX

Bare
branches
sway in the
wind — the
sun
dazzles.

The barren trees are swaying in the breeze
The grass is dry but it's not growing yet
It's warm today but it's kind of a tease
Spring is coming but it isn't here yet
Snow is approaching but there won't be much
There's no denying the sun's new dazzle
And snow will fall but I'm not caring much
As winter's grasp is becoming feeble
I'm looking forward to the bright fresh leaves
To the budding of the apple blossoms
I want to hear the wind tossing the leaves
I love crabapple and cherry blossoms
And it won't be long before we hear the frogs
The tree the chorus and the peeper frogs.

Spring leaves
in breezes
tumble
swell
soothe.

This could be a day in February
As it snowed last night and the sky is white
But the snow is only temporary
And most of it will be gone by tonight
I'm taking the time to enjoy the snow
As if I had never seen it before
Very soon the grass will begin to grow
And it won't be bitter cold anymore
The weight of winter is dissipating
I can feel a spring moisture in the air
Bright days are coming — I don't mind waiting
Gloom may be lingering but I don't care
So many winters have come and passed by
But I never tire of watching the sky.

Winter dissipating
river ice dissolving
birds and trees
grass and leaves
soon titillating.

My blackened toenails needed a year to
Grow out enough for me to clip off the
Damage that resulted from wearing shoes
The pinched my toes and it won't happen again

And I will traverse the countryside with
Jason again like we did last year and
He will take enormous bounding strides
At an arduous pace and I will struggle

To keep up and we will explore
Springtime resurrection again and
He will use ecological wisdom
To expose my ignorance and explode

My misapprehensions and I will be
Exhausted afterwards but satisfied.

And my toenails
afterwards will
remain pink and
pristine inside of
better shoes.

Jason sees a gaggle of geese and swans
Flying together in one formation
Jason understands the geese and the swans
Not surprised by their cooperation
He strides through William O'Brien State Park
And it's exhausting for me to keep up
He points out the Neolithic landmarks
After eleven miles he speeds up
He tells me about the various trees
He sees flowers that don't look like flowers
He has a mastery of the species
As I stride stomp and struggle for hours
Afterwards I know much more than I did
And my feet are aching and I'm done in.

For Jason every
season is not merely a
repetition of
of previous seasons but
a new origination.

We are lucky to find the ones in our
Lives who hear our words and intentions who
Have the persistence to see the layers
Of complexity and contradictions

And foibles and who accept and love us
With whom we in our turn may practice the
Skills of listening and of accepting
Our conflicting opinions and habits

Without recourse to coercive measures
As getting along harmoniously
Is a trick of compromise of letting
Go of expectations because the turns

Of circumstances will be jarring and
A loving partner is invaluable.

Whatever I think
will happen
probably won't
happen like that.

I didn't see the end coming and I'm
Sad we aren't a match but I'm grateful for
The conversation we shared drawing out
The pivotal experiences of

Our lives that made us the people we are
Today and I won't forget your kindness
And your probing intelligence — but you
Befuddled me by breaking it off so

Suddenly — and now you are teaching me
The lesson of how to let go without
Recrimination as I aspire
To be as light as a feather with the

People I love allowing emotions
To simmer freely and then to settle.

Letting emotions
come and go
without having to
figure them out
is excellent practice.

Taking a walk around a lake I see
The cattails along the shore that prospered
Last summer but now they're dried and lifeless
And I wonder how is it that these dead

Stalks will be removed and replaced by a
New generation as nature has a
Way of continuing and I feel and
Listen to the wind wrapping about me

And into my ears communicating
A sharp and eerie force of nature that
Chafes and chills as I encounter that which
Disintegrates forms and yet somehow makes

Possible the arising of other
Forms that flourish under a summer sun.

How shall I
characterize the wind —
indifferent
mournful
joyful?

There is so much happening when I step
Outside of my house with not a cloud in
The sky as the chilly air is like a
Moist tonic of spring liveliness bracing

And intoxicating and the air is
Filled with what seems celebratory
Birdsong of which I can identify
The irrepressible house finches but

There is a medley unknown to me
As the urgency and boisterous tunes
Of the birds overwhelm the gentle breeze
As the birds are invisible perching

In innumerable branches but their
Presence is impossible to ignore.

Is the urgency of
morning birdsong
of celebration or of
competition?

The male birds are moved in the morning to
Make their presence known to establish their
Territories and find mates which is an
Aggressive urgency that appears like

Celebration but is an assertion
Of strength and will as the primacy of
Mating fills these delicate creatures of
Feathers and bones living within their scope

Of a cosmos inaccessible to
Me but I have the detached pleasure of
Listening and of seeing the array
Of their plumage in happenstance glimpses

As I go about my business immersed
Within a world of conflicted thinking.

Open sky
swaying branches
singing birds are
a weaving of
cosmic becoming.

Walking away from another woman
After six months of companionship is
Not so easy as her manner of thought
And being were becoming enfolded

Within mine but the sudden break also came
With a sense of relief as I knew we
Were compatible in certain ways
And not so much in other ways and time

Was necessary to weigh whether
We could be together and my mind is
Recalling the words of encouraging
Enthusiasm we shared but also

The misgivings and reservations I
Felt that I suspect she was aware of.

Finding durable
compatibility
between complicated
singles is
tricky.

The crow is taken by the wind and blown
Across the sky tilting its wings letting
The forceful current of air overwhelm
Its intended direction pushed aside

From where it was going and it doesn't
Resist the wind but goes along with it
In harmony as the branches of the
Trees of the neighborhood are all swaying

Continuously in a spring uproar
As the first budding of the new leaves is
Becoming visible reviving a
Pattern of resurrection that I am

Familiar with but for the passing crow
Every spring must be a revelation.

I don't know where
the crow went as
it probably perched
in a tree within its
territory.

Outside of my portal of a window
Where I sit and type my poems as I'm
Watching the world there is a cottonwood
Tossing within a wind as a crow is

Perching on a branch bobbing its head and
Splaying and folding its tail feathers and
Flapping its wings and then it departs and
As I'm watching higher up several

Crows are determinedly forcing their way
Against the wind and a single crow is
Following behind and I'm reminded
Of the arrowhead formations of the

Geese that are evolved to efficiently
Cut through air by the thousands of miles.

The crows haven't
formed themselves
for the long haul of
migration — they
are homebodies.

On the thresholds of the Shinto shrines in
Japan there are standing tori gates which
Are the barest of structures comprising
Only two vertical posts — through which the

People enter the shrines — that are topped by
Two horizontal beams and the passage
Of the gates symbolizes the leaving
Behind of the ordinary and the

Entering of the sacred precinct of
The shrines and the gates are said to be the
Abodes of the birds and because I'm not
Japanese I may mistake their meaning

But I adore the idea that one
May take a step and enter into peace.

The gates are painted
vermilion a shade
of bright
loveliness.

I am a believer in the troughs and
Crests of life having experienced the
Intimacy and the solicitude
Of love for a time which I assumed would

Continue indefinitely and now
I know how it feels to have love withdrawn
Suddenly and seemingly without a
Reason and there's anger and hurt and a

Compulsion to figure out what happened
But really there's nothing to do but to
Receive the disorientation of
A loss which is a trough on the way to

Becoming a crest while accepting the
Traumatic quality of emotion.

Each personality
leaves ripples
merging into
incessant
undulation.

I went to match.com and renewed my
Membership and updated my profile
With a suggestion that women of a
Political persuasion probably

Wouldn't work for me because it's a fact
Today society is polarized
Into factions and even with people
Who don't like politics and who don't watch

The news their opinions are already
Cast in concrete and differing thought may
Spark a hair-trigger reaction maybe
Not today but eventually so

With bruising experience I've learned to
Sidestep trouble with preemptive phrasing.

Mating is
much less
complicated
for the birds.

The tripwires crossing society are in
Flux as I got a call from a retired
Coal miner in Ohio in response
To a sales letter I sent inviting

Subscriptions to a publication that
I operate and in conversation
He revealed divisions between the
Union leadership and the miners and

He talked about dishonesty and the
Difficulty of separating the
Facts from rhetoric and promises made
And based on a similarity of

Of opinion we found agreement that
The direction of the nation is bad.

No matter where
a person stands
the tripwires of
politics are
dangerous.

In the land of the Wiener schnitzel this
Animal was bred for hunting badgers
In dens so it has muscled front legs with
Sharp claws for digging in the earth and it

Is doggedly determined on a hunt
Possessing a pointy nose and sharp teeth
A barrel chest with plenty of heart for
A fight and it has a resonant bark

With soulful eyes and facial expressions
With a proud and a confident carriage
Being brave to the point of recklessness
And rumbustiously adorable but

The wiener dog is wary and jealous
So be careful because he may bite you.

The dachshund has
intelligent eyes
pleading for table scraps
which it shouldn't get
lest it become fat.

The wiener dog has pomp and dignity
It's not concerned about your opinion
In its own way it displays symmetry
It's not a dog of easy submission
The dachshund is intelligent and bold
Bred by the Germans for hunting badgers
Its trotting style is a sight to behold
And the dog has a mouth full of daggers
It is long of body and short of leg
The carriage of its head shows confidence
With strangers it may be a powder keg
It has an appetite that's bottomless
And the dog may beg with very sad eyes
But tossing it table scraps is unwise.

The wiener dog is sporty
The wiener dog is snippy
its trotting along
is worthy of song
The wiener dog is perky.

Maybe it's better to be ignorant
And ignore political opinion
To slide by and become indifferent
And avoid the difficult decisions
But I'm not passive and I care too much
That politics today is dangerous
I'd like to discourse with a feather's touch
But so many topics are treacherous
We are spoon-fed nonstop accusation
Politicos purposely polarize
They profit from flammable gyrations
They hone their messages to demonize
The media is used to hypnotize
With the cruel intention to brutalize.

Lawyers and judges
law enforcement bureaucrats
the educators
and the media people
are all bitter partisans.

The issues are like Russian nesting dolls
Each of the dolls appears differently
A difference in knowledge makes a wall
Without knowledge there is no sympathy
The biggest doll is the news narrative
Partisan journalism isn't true
News is emotional and addictive
There is much dishonesty to sort through
Each doll presents greater complexity
The range of opinion is tremendous
Involving the context and history
And a lively debate could be endless
But the smallest doll is about power
And the truth about politics is sour.

Rules for Radicals
by Saul Alinsky and
The Prince
by Machiavelli
reveal the various tricks.

What do we mean when we say "consciousness"?
Does it include what we do while sleeping?
Is it just a measure of thoughtfulness?
Does everything have it if it's living?
I look at turkey vultures and eagles
Watching how they drift and soar with the wind
I listen to the mournful calls of gulls
Are they outside or inside of my mind?
I do some things of which I'm not aware
I am breathing lungs and beating a heart
Circulating blood and growing my hair
Am I one with the earth or set apart?
There is the weightiness of emotions
As imponderable as the oceans.

Do I separate
what happens
from how I respond?

The conference in Dallas launches on a
Friday evening with a cocktail hour which
Is challenging for me because I am
A stranger to everyone and I am

Compelled with the task of imposing
And introducing myself to people
Who know each other and who are engaged
In coteries of conversation as

They stand imbibing exhilarating
Drinks sporting their prestigious status and
Exchanging clubby insider's language
And awkwardly I do barge into a

Threesome smiling and showing off my teeth
Doing my best to be intelligent.

Polite society
is loaded with
tricks of
inclusion and
exclusion.

I heard a computer engineer talk
To a neurobiologist about
Artificial Intelligence and of
The potential dangers of runaway

Mechanical calculations made by
Hyperactive computers engendered
By humans that could only be held in
Check by competing platforms of "A. I."

Wherein if one system does establish
Preeminence then that entity would
Eliminate all competitors and
Lead to the subjugation of or the

Extinction of humanity which does
Imply that predation is foreordained.

The engineer seems
an updated version
of Dr. Frankenstein
touting the latest
silicon monster.

On Sunday morning the desk clerk called a
Taxi to the airport for me and on
His arrival the driver took my bag
And swung it into the trunk and on the

Ride he said his name was Sam and that
He missed driving in New York City and
He asked if I heard the speech from the
Rich man last night and I didn't know who

He was referring to and he said that
The Dallas airport is the only one
That charges taxis coming and going
And when we arrived the meter was on

Fifty dollars but he mumbled something
And then he charged me one hundred dollars.

I was caught off guard but I
have his name and cab number
and will claw back a refund
from Yellow Cab and
withdraw the tip.

A surge of power presses my body
As the engines roar along the runway
Speed is intensifying mightily
As the weight of my body falls away
As the airliner's wheels are lifting off
A thrust of power is precipitous
The plane is ascending steeply aloft
The engine's roaring is continuous
Pressure on my ears is making them pop
Something feels different but I'm not sure what
I'm feeling the blood in my temples throb
My seatbelt is locked and I'm staying put
The view from the window is amazing
The earth far below the clouds is moving.

Stuck in my seat
I'm reading a novel
waiting patiently
for a bottle of water
almonds and a biscuit.

The wind is taking me in sudden bursts
Testing the balance of the bicycle
It comes in roaring overwhelming spurts
But I can make it more manageable
I have to tame my appetite for speed
Because the wind is much stronger than me
Setting a gentle pace is what I need
The motion is easy and I'm carefree
It's exciting with the wind at my back
Now I'm speeding as fast as a greyhound
The time passes quickly and I lose track
My animal spirit is quite unbound
Spring is coming and the trees are budding
Today is joyous — the sunlight stunning.

The rippling river
far below the bridge
reflects sky and clouds —
the wind batters me
and the gulls.

I am sitting at a window and a
Desk watching the world parade by at
A pace that isn't lackadaisical
Or hurried seeing a puff of a cloud

Transforming in a northwesterly wind
When I see on the hedge four feet away
The birds that Fran had told me about that
I had never knowingly seen — redpolls —

And there is a male with splashes of red
About its chest and head and a female
Turning their heads and moving in jerky
Motions and I could have been lost thinking

About the taxi driver who tried to
Cheat me but instead I see the birds.

Beyond thought the
world is parading
neither rushed nor
lackadaisical.

Fran pointed out the difference between
The flights of turkey vultures and eagles
As the gliding of the wings of eagles
Is flat and the wings of the vultures have

More of a V shape and just a few words
Has improved my clarity of view and
Though the added insight doesn't give me
An ounce of leverage over people

It does impart a touch of pleasure as
I can see a little better into
The ceaseless parading of the earth as
Branches with emerging buds are swaying

In blusters and a few clouds are drifting
Southward at a pace that isn't harried.

The earth is wiggly
within a procession
of cyclical emergence
and disappearance.

It's easy to miss how lucky we are
Just stare at the news to become depressed
The propaganda they push is bizarre
Consume too much and you will be confused
Indulging anger is a sad mistake
I know because I've done it quite often
Resentment produces only heartache
I'd rather my emotions be softened
There is a vast world beyond my thinking
Occasionally I holiday there
Spring is coming and the trees are waking
And jubilant birdsong is in the air
Thought follows thought follows thought —
It's so easy to get tied up in knots.

Breath follows
breath follows
breath — it's
a better rhythm
to attend to.

It's April 1st and I'm feeling lazy
The snow is all gone and the sky is blue
Playing with words is a little crazy
I am sure there's something better to do
It's too chilly to ride my bicycle
I'm at my desk looking out my window
Just doing nothing isn't radical
It is better than playing pachinko
Oh well I lost a girlfriend poor poor me
I am just too weary to change her mind
There are advantages to being free
I can play with words if I'm so inclined
There are parts of me I don't want to change
So it's a better deal to disengage.

I am lackadaisical
with love drifting along
listening to bird song
too lazy to
move.

We ex-drunks meet in the park for our talk
Leveraging our sobriety while
Watching the sun rising and the vultures
Circling in the air as I stand freezing

My ears realizing sometimes it takes
More than a little adversity to
Summon the willingness to overcome
Self-pity and resentment coming so

Easily and afterward I rush home to
Fill my two containers with coffee and
I drive to the office preparing to
Drop into my chair eager to futz with

Words but then I realize that my phone
Is charging at home and that I need it.

Mornings are so
intoxicating that
sometimes details
escape me.

A scrap of information confided
Casually by a friend altered my
Everyday mind and now I am seeing
Differently what I had misperceived

Repeatedly so I am grateful to
Fran who revealed that they aren't eagles
But turkey vultures effortlessly and
Continuously singly or in wakes that

Are exploiting the thermal currents of
Air and without the circling of the birds
The quality of the restless air would
Be invisible and so I wonder

What else is eluding me — what else is
Over the horizon of my knowing.

I am only
sixty-three years old
and have plenty
of time left.

Let's have fun with innocent malaprops
I want to dance with you the flamingo
Let's have popcorn and watch an agitprop
A most lovely bird is the flamenco
The English language is full of riddles
The same vowels are spelled so differently
My handwriting is an awful scribble
I'm not capable of calligraphy
As I kid I was inarticulate
No one's ideal of virtuosity
I wasn't suspected of intelligence
And had not a hint of verbosity
But now I am old and full of whimsy
Don't give a damn — and my ego's flimsy.

Trouble comes from
being serious —
nonsense is
easy.

I would like my mind to be like a bowl
And to accept with grace phenomenon
To be happy to observe a redpoll
Or whatever birds I happen upon
But I get bogged down with controversy
And there is no end of trouble and strife
A head full of resentments is messy
Like cutting off toes with a butcher knife
Trying to make sense is a loser's game
If I try too hard I'm certain to fail
There is always someone that I can blame
With plenty of meatheads to put in jail
Writing doggerel is a saving grace
Much better than packing a can of mace.

There are always
birds flitting by
fitting in my
brain bowl
perfectly.

Whoever said that nonsense was easy?
All sensibility is pushed aside
I try to be just a little crazy
And assert a posture that's quite cockeyed
I may be lusty and may be lazy
Neither fastidious nor dignified
When learning the rules I may be hazy
Of formalities I am horrified
I'd like to see an African daisy
As long as I'm sure it is bonafide
And I'd love to savor bouillabaisse
But green pea soup I really can't abide
I like to loiter and come in with the tide
Don't have expectations — I may backslide.

This rhyming
business is just
abysmal
fizzle and
piffle.

There are Zen koans in which the monks are
Challenged to take Mount Fuji out of a
Pill box or to pull the four divisions
Of Tokyo out of a sleeve of a

Kimono and I don't pretend to know
The answer to these riddles that the monks
Grappled with to the point of despair but
As I look out of the window seeing

The same trees that are here day after day
And feel the upholding support that the
Chair is giving me I make a bubble
Of warm oxygen about myself and

Notice the gravitational tug of
The event horizon of a black hole.

Holding a closed fist
and persuading a child
there's something inside —
such are the riddles of
Zen.

The absence of a girlfriend is tricky
I do appreciate conversation
My expectations aren't a bit picky
And splitting up has brought a deflation
But I'm not unhappy to be alone
Now I don't have to match her schedule
I'm not spending so much time on the phone
Twining my thoughts with hers was typical
It's true I need others to be healthy
I do want a person to bounce off of
Do I want to be controlled? Not really
I'll find another way of doing love
My home is like a Zen monastery
Where probing my thought is salutary.

Nonsensical
utterance with
Kitcat keeps the
house lively.

The wiener dog is a noble creature
He doesn't care that his legs are so short
For self-confidence he is my teacher
His comportment upon the earth is stout
Looking at him you would think that he "yips"
But instead he has a mighty dog's bark
With his barrel chest he can let 'er rip
And he also has the teeth of a shark
It's said he is a good family dog
As he begs at dinner for table scraps
With such sad eyes he starts a dialogue
But his persuasive eyes are only traps
You shouldn't give in because he'll get fat
So please don't be responsible for that.

The unselfconscious
trotting gait of
the wiener dog
bespeaks dignity.

Animals are lucky that they don't think
They don't cultivate weighty opinions
Their vision and impulses are in sync
They don't agonize over decisions
They're not wasting any time on mirrors
They couldn't care less about self-image
They don't do their own accounting figures
They're not scornful — they don't do patronage
A hippo is ugly but doesn't care
Elephants are wise but they don't worry
A deer endures losses but doesn't swear
An aging lion doesn't feel sorry
Humans are burdened with conflicting thoughts
We tie ourselves in complicated knots.

But there's poignancy
and redemption in
simplifying
burdened
thought.

Seeds of the poem are in the first line
Only a hint will make a beginning
And fibrous roots become curious twine
This open moment is worth exploring
Ideas may be lively and playful
Syllables take on rhythm and meaning
My inspiration tends to be grateful
Don't know what I am anticipating
Might I journey in any direction?
Line after line compels a commitment
I like the subtlety of inflection
Looking back I can see I'm consistent
Sincerity of purpose will evoke
An acorn creates a mighty bur oak.

I could have been
a resentful drunk —
today I cultivate
hints of
possibility.

Buds of the trees are irrepressible
Sunlight is becoming solicitous
This lively season is unquenchable
But I do feel a little wistfulness
Air in spring is quite intoxicating
I won't allow myself to be inside
Is it my heart or the sun pulsating?
Though after a while I am getting fried
As I have lived though many springs before
And each one appears a resurrection
But I am really not young anymore
And can't stop my having circumspection
The spring is always extrasensory
And I carry a weight of memory.

Apple blooms are
on the way while the
intimacy I've known
has gone away.

There is a chemistry between people
An ease of comfort or nervous tension
As our experience isn't equal
Which affects our manner of expression
There are two women of my acquaintance
With each one I behave differently
With one I exhibit loving patience
With the other verbal dexterity
Each one elicits a version of me
And with both I'm being true to myself
I am behaving spontaneously
They are also genuinely themselves
Without you I don't know who I could be
I discover you and you unfold me.

Alone with my
thoughts so much
of my thinking is
conversation
reverberating.

Rhyming is a game so don't expect much
It's not really serious but it's fun
I want to imitate a feather's touch
Before you notice the poem is done
Just being sensible can be messy
What can I do with galloping nonsense?
And can I make my proofreaders fussy?
Correcting faulty grammar can be tense
Sometimes I think that I'm wasting my time
There are productive chores to be doing
I could be putting on a pantomime
Then I wouldn't have to write anything
But rhyming and fooling can be handy
Reducing today to cotton candy.

It's tricky to make a pun
Only for a bit of fun
Ignoring my work
And going berserk
And suddenly I am done.

It's a shame that I have to be wary
That often it's better to be quiet
Politics these days has gotten scary
And it's necessary to be private
I thrive on intellectual questions
I like to parse the various issues
But want to do it without aggression
The need for honest debate continues
But I've never seen such intolerance
It's easy to be smeared as a "hater"
But it's vile a mass of incoherence
With worse consequences coming later
The media is revolutionized
Public discussions have been brutalized.

I'd like to think
friendships are immune
to political pressures
but it's better not to
test.

It is clever to make accusations
Hurling narratives of collective guilt
It's a crafty form of misdirection
As the opposition cowers and wilts
Groups of people are said to be hateful
Based on perceptions of race or gender
While the accusers themselves are spiteful
And guilty of what they say of others
Trained activists are making the charges
Accusing innocent working people
The supposed solutions are mirages
The hatred created may be lethal
It is a dirty dishonest system
Persuading people that they are victims.

Leverage comes from
accusing the innocent
and directing
an army of
angry victims.

America is in turmoil today
Even in the midst of prosperity
Our trust in each other is giving way
We don't appreciate our luxuries
And we are shredding our institutions
Cops are suspects of criminal intent
Celebrities call for prosecution
There are surging rages of discontent
Controversies are splintering our schools
Is America an evil nation?
We can't agree on societal rules
The news is full of rabid gyrations
And public discourse dispenses venom
Every news cycle is now a weapon.

Disconnecting from
the news isn't a
protection from
societal drift.

Resentment is a terrible master
Inspiring malignant obsessions
An attractive trick for news broadcasters
Spurring the viewers' latent aggressions
The news depicts the plight of victimhood
Seizing events and forming narratives
But pivotal details aren't understood
Shaping opinion is imperative
Scorn is focused on the perpetrators
Those whom the media want to destroy
Reporters assume the role of saviors
Directing hate is a lucrative ploy
Humans have an appetite for anger
It seems an unappeasable hunger.

Am I not as guilty
as those whom I
accuse? Escaping
resentment is
tricky.

Life doesn't fit in simple narratives
Choices are a maze of complexity
It's not helpful to be comparative
Much better to consider empathy
Resentment is a terrible poison
It's not worth the self-consuming fury
Even for justifiable reasons
It makes all other emotions heavy
But the pain of resentment helped me change
I had to learn the art of letting go
Mistrusting my own thoughts at first was strange
I had to cultivate a faith and grow
I suffered a measure of frustration
Enough to desire liberation.

Resenting is like
setting my own house
on fire and
refusing to
escape.

A steady rain has dominated for
The last several days with the persisting
Sunlight being filtered through the gloom of
Dark gray clouds but I can't help rejoicing

Because the grass is greening with new growth
As the frost is gone and the soil is moist
And I've washed and put away my winter
Fleeces and the branches of the trees that

I've watched through the bitter cold are budding
With incipient leaves and the croaking
Of frogs is mixing with the sounds of the
Birds and yes there are moments when the light

Of day suddenly dims with the threat of
Impending rain but this is all joyous.

The complexity
of human entanglements
vanishes once the
prospect of pedaling on
my bicycle returns.

We hadn't seen Steve since the beginning
Of the pandemic a year ago but
He showed at the park for our meeting as
Curmudgeonly as usual with more

Gray hair than before and looking worn by
The separation imposed by the fear of
Catching the virus which has lifted from
Him as he is vaccinated now and

Is reclaiming his place among us in his
Turn speaking honestly and assessing
How he's doing remarking that it seems
Like years have passed but then as we regain

Familiarity it seems only a
Couple of weeks since we've ruminated.

Separation
and reunion
vaguely hint
at evolving
personality.

Everyone has issues with family
Or coworkers or friends going on right
Now as somebody's not happy be it
A birthday party that's not wanted or

The disturbance of moving domiciles
Whatever can be wrung through the wringer
Of ceaseless adaptation brutally
And minutely as things are changing for

Better or worse and it's too bad normal
People aren't as sick as alcoholics
Who either disintegrate or practice
Principles to be sober because the

Normally agitated could learn a
Lot from our hilarious bantering.

Every meeting is
a festival of
disruptive
frivolity.

My mom asked about which are the things in
The house that I would like to inherit
And there are many items connected
With memory but I'm at a time when

I'd rather empty my own house of most
Of what I consider as the debris
Of my grown and gone family and I'd
Prefer my living space to embody

A bare simplicity of artful and
Useful implements that are a pleasure
To hold in my hands with the rooms being
An uncluttered arrangement allowing

For the unhindered playing of my mind
Free of the past and untroubled today.

I will take the sturdy
oak rocking chair
that positions
a body
alertly.

My dad used to
sit in the oak chair
rocking watching
football on Sundays.

Everything I do especially the
Composing of pithy poems comes with
A natural human propensity
For measuring and balancing as the

Satisfaction I take in symmetry
Gives me a sense of the mastery of
My surroundings and by assuming the
Task of organizing the lines of words

In ten syllables while also crafting
A flow of rhythm overrunning the
Ends of lines without superfluous words
Brings a feeling of accomplishment as

If I were a finicky mason
Assembling a beautiful wall of stones.

Self-referential
arbitrary choice
emerges into
a regimented
clever expression.

The gesturing of the trees cuts against
The grain of my innate preference for
Measure and symmetry opposing my
Human habits of regularity

With an explosion of angles and crooks
As I gaze at the massive cottonwood
On my corner season after season
And yet the twists and turns of it defy

My comprehension of it as when I
Close my eyes and attempt to capture a
View of it only the vaguest image
Comes to mind as its form surpasses my

Ability to fix and grab ahold
Of — and every single tree is like that.

The trees
grow themselves
wild and
incomprehensible.

The sun is bright this morning after days
Of dominating gray clouds dispensing
Rain and gloom leaving puddles in the low
Areas of my driveway and there are

Hundreds of drops of water hanging from
The crooked branches of my apple tree
With each drop dangling gleaming with sunlight
With the grass glistening reflecting the

Rising sun and though the forecast points to
A continuation of such stormy
And chilly weather for the coming week
Even for a reappearance of snow

Tomorrow buds of leaves are appearing
And the grass is green and growing again.

Clinging gloom on the
undeniable
threshold of spring
moisture brings me
barely suppressed joy.

A sound in the woods is gurgling again
Water is moving over ground again
Collecting itself into creeks and streams
Making its ways along channels down to

The river again clean water coming
From the springs and the saturated earth
Flowing over and around and moving
The smallest of stones about and rounding

The hard edges of the stones persisting
Among the heavy stones and the boulders
Giving the woods a musical patter
Of frolicsome splashing and pouring and

Water has been moving on the earth for
Eons without a lick of memory.

Water doesn't remember
oceans clouds drops
mist fog springs creeks
streams rivers valleys
canyons deltas.

Not every thought I have is worth my time
So many are habitual nonsense
It is an exuberant game to rhyme
Which demands a little reconnaissance
And words resemble a workingman's tools
With usage comes familiarity
It does take practice to master the rules
There is play in verbal dexterity
Mastering facts is the goal of science
And I sprinkle my poems with the truth
Truth and whimsy may make an alliance
Much better than having a wisdom tooth
It is easy to get lost in my head
I'd much rather juggle with words instead.

Every day I am thinking
And my spirits are sinking
But I can waste time
Attempting to rhyme
And I will end up winking.

One is pronounced a hippopotamus
While two are termed as hippopotami
But it's different with rhinoceros
Because we do not say "rhinoceri"
Words are wiggly and they make me weary
There are many ways to spell the vowels
Thankfully we do have dictionaries
Otherwise I would very often scowl
I use the words but didn't invent them
English has become an awful mishmash
What is the logic behind the word "phlegm"?
Thinking too much will summon a whiplash
Who coined the happy word "propitious"?
It is useful for being facetious.

Words are indispensable
They make the world sensible
If I couldn't talk
I would have to squawk
Which isn't delectable.

April in Minnesota is crazy
We just enjoyed days of summery heat
With humidity that made me lazy
Followed by these days of wintery sleet
The buds are growing and the grass is green
I expect that tulips are on the way
The leaves will have an incandescent sheen
But today the sky is a mass of gray
And I am seeing snow on every roof
And my bicycle has gotten a flat
So it's not hard for me to stand aloof
At least we're not swatting at swarming gnats
Temperate weather arrives when it does
April's as crazy as it ever was.

My bicycle tire is fixed
I've ordered new tires
and a bicycle
computer for
mileage and speed.

The news is heavy with tragic events
A police shooting has happened again
Convulsing America with suspense
Because riots are happening again
People are divided by what they see
We are forming into suspicious groups
Our differing narratives don't agree
But who are justified and who are dupes?
Few can counter the tides of history
The Buddha said that the world is burning
Why tragedy comes is a mystery
We are angry and the streets are burning
The best I can do is watch and let go
Society is always full of woe.

I don't know how
liberation comes
but I'm pretty sure
not from anger.

I googled "leafless gutters" because the
Wire mesh isn't keeping the debris
From the trees about my house from clogging
My gutters and I found the website of

A company in Colorado that
Offers leafless gutters and handyman
Services too which I also wanted
Because a bush needs to be removed to

Make way for a downspout that's presently
Blocked leading to water leaking into
My basement so I scheduled a date for
Services and entered my credit card

Information and I was happy that
I had addressed a critical problem.

This morning I am
seized with suspicion
that I used a website
to swindle myself
with naiveté.

I realize the process dispensed with
A meeting with a sales rep who would make
An estimate of the costs and price which
Would be necessary for a proper

Deal and I am seized with revulsion that
I stupidly allowed myself to be
Swindled by a website in cyberspace
Without a telephone number so I

Call my credit card company and learn
That the charge hasn't yet happened and with
Relief I cancel the card to stop the
Payment redeeming my ineptitude —

I only wasted time in frustration
In which I could have written poetry.

I could have
written wonderful
poetry if I hadn't
been distracted.

By myself on the way to Amsterdam
I remember the White Cliffs of Dover
Taking the ferry and the trains and trams
I found a love I've not gotten over
Inside of a book of Shakespeare's sonnets
I was a lonely student at Oxford
Seeking love in solitary moments
Feeling emotions that didn't accord
I was piqued by his pitiful laments
By his lusty and cloying strategy
And by his utterly sincere pretense
With metaphorical rascality
But most of all I loved his playful words
And everything else was kind of absurd.

I admired the hearty
way Shakespeare had
of making words flow
and resonate.

Shakespeare was a superior playwright
But in sonnets he became an actor
Assuming the role of a lover's plight
Striking poses of impassioned fracture
He was in love with someone much younger
And much lamented his impending death
Implying unappeasable hunger
Dreading the expiration of his breath
He contrived to make his lover guilty
By pretending to let his lover go
Slighting himself — soliciting pity
And then he turned to braggadocio
Deploying all the tricks that words can do
Plotting to finagle a rendezvous.

While I waited for a train
in Amsterdam Shakespeare
cast a spell on me.

I could let my mind drift away with clouds
They are wispy and moving south today
They often cover the sky like a shroud
But I could let the clouds take me away
The trees are an enticing counterpoint
Without a wind they stand so peacefully
They're an infinity of crooks and joints
They are expressing themselves quietly
I love to watch the procession of light
Seeing contrails of a jetliner drift
It's easy to discount the joys of sight
And to forget that my eyes are a gift
But so much thinking goes on in my head
I get stuck in controversy instead.

I am not free of
the compulsion
to organize myself
and make decisions.

I'd rather not be guarded with my words
Because I love easy conversation
But it's true I am a bit of a nerd
And can't meet everyone's expectations
With certain people I discuss the news
But with some those topics are out of bounds
Because we have to share similar views
Otherwise there's too much trouble around
If you ask me I'll tell you what I think
And I'm sure it would be enjoyable
It is joyous to find ourselves in sync
But first I'd like you to be flexible
I don't insist that we need to agree
But I desire the grace to be carefree.

With some people
I can sense a brick wall
existing behind
their eyes.

Saturday is an oasis for me
When I sit at my desk writing poems
Being as nonsensical as I please
Typing my lines of rambunctious hokum
I had a girlfriend much smarter than me
I would visit her about once a week
But we couldn't agree ultimately
So now we're separate and we don't speak
I don't really know what happened that day
Suddenly she was unhappy with me
I expect I'll find another someday
One who's much less complicated maybe
Saturday is free — I do what I want
It's easy for me to be nonchalant.

Shakespeare made
such a big deal out of love
but I am suspicious —
was it all an act?

So much of life is indescribable
There is only so much that words can do
The forms of the trees are ineffable
Can't always explain what I think is true
The sun and the clouds are quite beautiful
But can't exactly articulate why
Consciousness is incomprehensible
I try to think but my thoughts go awry
Will I go to sleep and never wake up?
Did I come to the earth from somewhere else?
I am confused — will I ever grow up?
Is this all that there is — with nothing else?
How much am I free to think what I want?
I can relax with a buttered croissant.

A single cloud is
transforming in
the sky at a
gentle pace.

Let these pages enfold my memory
I don't want to feel the weight anymore
I don't remember very cleverly
What I recall I would rather ignore
What stands out is painful experience
All the things that I would like to forget
All the disappointed reminiscence
Let me skillfully use the alphabet
I will give my essence to these pages
Let my memory be within this book
And let the book be the one that ages
I can fashion out a witty scrapbook
I want to be smartly spontaneous
Like the sky itself — momentaneous.

The sky doesn't remember
yesterday as it's awake and
liberated.

Actors know the power of their faces
They reflect the subtlest emotions
Sincerity and empathy graces
Expressing that which remains unspoken
They say so much with a cast of their eyes
Summoning pity with tremulous lips
Utterly convincing when telling lies
It's hard to believe they're following scripts
They must embody emotions themselves
Feeling the sadness and disappointment
Adopting the aggressions that compel
With authenticity being poignant
I have to wonder who they really are
Doing what's needed to become a star.

The best actors
don't overplay
but genuinely
express what's
put on.

Do I really desire to fall in love?
Or is it best to encourage friendship?
Do I want a lover's passion? Sort of
Perhaps it's best to have companionship
But do I want the grip of obsession?
I know what it's like to become consumed
Nagging jealousy comes with possession
A desperate attachment is perfumed
Observe what love did to William Shakespeare
Love made him gesticulate like a fool
Emotions are hard — especially fear
And rejection can seem utterly cruel
So I don't know what will happen to me
And all I can do is to wait and see.

Romantic love
isn't gentle — it's
like being run over
by a Mack truck.

Kitcat is expert at rascality
But I can't say that he's a deep thinker
He likes to show off his dexterity
When evading my grasp he's a slinker
He's crafty at grabbing my attention
He'll knock containers off the kitchen counter
Then he'll look at me with expectation
Wanting to spark a nutty encounter
But I don't chase I just expostulate
I stay on the couch while waving my arms
I'm often pretending to be irate
But I'm sure that he knows I mean no harm
He's not very brainy but is a clown
Making me grateful that he is around.

While he lays on his back
we slap and swat
hands and paws
and he tries to bite
while I sing nonsense.

They often come about the size of peas
But once in a while they're elephantine
Then I am surprised and certainly pleased
So weighty with juice and tasting so fine
They're shipped to America from Chile
Which really is a modern miracle
They're not necessary — but are frilly
And they do make my breakfast magical
I combine their flavor with banana
I do love my exotic morning fruit
I sprinkle both upon my granola
They give my appetite a mighty toot
They come here — even in February
What would I do without my blueberries?

The skim milk
that completes
the ensemble is
pleasingly
bland.

Early in the morning while passing an
Ash tree I notice about a dozen
Turkey vultures at the top of a tree
With several of them spreading out their wings

And I observe that that particular
Tree that I pass every day has about
It a disheveled appearance because
Its branches and twigs are extending in

A weirdly chaotic fashion — so here
Are these strange birds with a six-foot wingspan
Gathered together quietly perching
In an odd-looking tree and I don't know

What the birds are thinking but I'm amazed
To see such an assemblage of beings.

When I keep my eyes open
and my mind quiet
even in my own
neighborhood the
world surprises me.

Imagine being a photon of light
Zipping away from a supernova
Exhalation of energy at the
Speed of light — I wonder whether as a

Particular particle I would have
A sensation of motion noticing
Galaxies zooming by for billions of
Years with neither acceleration nor

Diminution of impetus or would
There be an absence of a sense of time
As my arriving and departing are
Simultaneous instantaneous

As there would no longer be time or space
For a ham sandwich and a tomato.

In
reality
my
neighborhood
is
odd.

Might I politely have your attention
And persuade you to come together with
Me skipping along over syllables
Lazily and lackadaisically

As I hint at a truth advantageous
And propitious for you to absorb
Not that I'm the only person privy
To the inside scoop as it's a fact as

Common as a heartbeat as it's a trick
Of directing oneself away from the
Habituated run of the mind so
Often chewing over useless thinking

Serving only for agitation — you
Should be wary of knowing the news.

The news isn't
only informing
but also skewing
opinions and
emotions.

I'm not an advocate of ignorance
As the human mind is incapable
Of avoiding the cultivation of
Opinions which quite naturally are

Prickly and neither am I bestowing
Wishy-washy attitudes upon you
As we can't help digging into things as
Determinedly as a wiener dog but

I am reminding myself and also
Suggesting to you it's good at times to
Lovingly propagate the emptiness
Of the sky allowing the thunderclouds

And lightning due exercise while also
Remaining open and spontaneous.

The open sky
receives the weather
of the world but
holds on to
nothing.

In the grip of daily habit I drive
About Stillwater letting the chatter
Of the radio provide me with the
Political opinion that I like

Aware of the toxicity coming
With my opinions of issues over
Which I have no measure of influence
And I often become weary as the

Controversy never ceases and for
An escape I've taken to observing
The various posturing of the trees
As a tonic and an antidote as

They are visions of spontaneity
Separate from human contrivances.

Trees do have
patterns of specie
but they are
infinitely
various.

When my energy wanes and peters out
My attitude is unreliable
I discover myself consumed with doubt
My ambitions are unbelievable
Then I compare my progress with others
Seeing I lack the friends that many have
That I haven't had my share of lovers
And then my battered ego needs a salve
But this has happened many times before
I know such thoughts are unreliable
So I don't debate myself anymore
And harmony is unsustainable
Energy naturally ebbs and flows
I don't punish myself when I am low.

Surfing
melancholy
is easier.

I am out of step with fashion today
Poets now are revolutionary
I don't want the outrage that they convey
Prefer to avoid verbal savagery
I do not believe in collective guilt
Quite distrust their poisonous narratives
I'd rather compose a different script
Can't be so resolutely negative
But poets are out of fashion also
No one reads poetry much anymore
Can poets make money? I don't think so
We aren't celebrated in the bookstores
Don't really care that I'm out of fashion
I write poetry for satisfaction.

I
love
to
make
the
words
dance.

Does Shakespeare comport with Japanese Zen?
Elizabethan poems are wordy
The bard wrote with honeyed metaphors then
English poetry is much more heady
The Japanese are sparing with their words
They don't invest so much in verbiage
And yet they are effective with their verbs
They slice delusion with a razor's edge
Zen is a practice based on clarity
And Japanese poetry is concise
I admire Shakespeare's dexterity
And in his wordiness he is precise
Emulating both may just be crazy
Whatever I do can't be lazy.

I adore
Matsuo
Basho's
frog jumping
into a temple
pond.

I do my best to be open to life
To forget the burdens of yesterday
To forge of myself a very keen knife
And slice through the troubles along my way
But I know I can't function on my own
That life is better when someone loves me
That people don't prosper living alone
That it is healthy for us to agree
I want to grasp hold of true perceptions
And to minimize my own disturbance
To take ownership of my selections
To be balanced in every occurrence
We are thrust on the point of becoming
And something propitious is coming.

I can't see
around corners
and can only
clarify me.

I am grateful to see hypocrisy
As it shows me clearly what not to do
Some are brazen in their mendacity
But it's sometimes hard to see as I do
Opinions vary and we don't agree
We come at things from various angles
That it's hard to know the truth — I concede
Omniscience is given to angels
There is a tinge to denunciations
A tactile hint of falsification
Making me question their accusations
They are broadcasting a mad delusion
And the hypocrites are always angry
Which sooner or later summons gangrene.

A person has to watch
for contradictory
behavior over time
to spot hypocrisy.

The sky has the virtue of emptiness
Its true quality is invisible
Its conversion is instantaneous
Always spontaneously flexible
A cloudless sky isn't really empty
The life of the sunlight is pouring down
Soliciting oxygen from the trees
The stars are visible after sundown
And winter is often shrouded with clouds
Then the earth is saturated with rain
And in summer the thunderheads resound
In every season sunlight comes again
But the sky itself is not the weather
It's the emptiness holding the weather.

The cosmos is not
galaxies and time
it is emptiness holding
galaxies and time.

In the winter I wrote about tulips
Because it's good to be optimistic
So I imagined the blooming tulips
Lifting my mood by being artistic
It's been a chilly and a dreary spring
Had I known I'd have been disappointed
I can't predict what the future will bring
It's very easy to be downhearted
But it's rainy today and I don't care
I am even quite enthusiastic
What comes today I can easily bear
I am doing spiritual gymnastics
Cavorting with words will lighten my mood
Without playing tricks my life would be skewed.

By the garage
today I see
red and yellow tulips
come up simultaneously
with daffodils.

In Washington D.C. cherry trees bloom
During the warm early days of April
But how can anyone escape the gloom
At the site of national betrayal?
In Japan they celebrate plum blossoms
That appear in February and March
They are such sweet and delicate blossoms
When beauty and the end of winter merge
And in Japan they enjoy Golden Week
Which happens within the first week of May
Everyone celebrates which is unique
As the cherry blossoms brighten their days
And also in May wisteria comes
When purple flowers exquisitely bloom.

The Japanese bestowed
the gift of cherry trees
on Washington D.C. —
the city of our
political disease.

Most of April has been damp and soggy
Puddles are collecting on my driveway
My apple trees are barren and gnarly
They don't blossom until the end of May
Giving me something to look forward to
I've mowed the lawn but it's growing slowly
And outside now I don't have much to do
At least it's unlikely to be snowy
I love my lilac bush and apple trees
When they bloom I quietly celebrate
And I welcome seeing the bumblebees
Spring comes in Minnesota — it's not late
My wiry lilac bush and apple trees
Determinedly persist through the deep freeze.

In late May the scent
of lilac and apple
blossoms mingle
over my yard
for about a week.

A downpour spattering on the concrete
Along with bamboo knocking together
Such a welcome release from sticky heat
That all these years later I remember
We were lying near the open window
Wrapped in warm blankets upon our futons
A married couple living in Kyoto
With so much youthful drama going on
It's a memory of a vanished time
Of the sensations that return to me
Of my own emotional pantomime
Remembering is important to me
There was so much life ahead of us then
I'd love to have the time over again.

Some
memories
abide
and I
don't know
why.

The alphabet is sophisticated
It gives the language organization
Sounds and meanings can be regulated
With dictionaries for definitions
Takes so much time to get educated
I've learned the grammatical conventions
A thrust of culture is indicated
A system aiding my comprehension
Eventually I've graduated
Discover myself in competition
Our society is complicated
Producing a little hypertension
I admit to my share of pretension
And I may even foster dissension.

Gazing at the
wild gesticulation
of the trees is an
antidote to
human thought.

How do you measure your velocity?
Do you enjoy an appetite for speed?
Do you have time for curiosity?
Is finishing early a worthy need?
Who could resist youthful precocity?
Is desire unambiguously greed?
What is the source of generosity?
Do you embody unknowable seeds?
Is there advantage in ferocity?
What does an obsessive ambition feed?
What is the goal of reciprocity?
Does genuine unselfish love succeed?
Is there any use in loquacity?
Or is it only harmless verbosity?

You may think you are
stationary but really
you are moving at
one thousand miles an hour
rotating upon the earth.

I admire a writer who scolded me
He was a professor but gave it up
He's intelligent and can be cranky
He loves literature with no letup
With his family he moved to Vermont
Choosing to live a simple farming life
A genuinely naïve dilettante
They struggled to survive — he and his wife
They started out as hippie homesteaders
Indulging whimsy — not experience
Now they are clever and weathered farmers
Overcoming hardships with resilience
All his life he's been writing and reading
And I find his opinions compelling.

I disparaged rhyming
and he chided me
remarking rhyming makes
remembering poetry
easier.

I dislike the revolutionaries
Because of their conceit that they know best
Believing as they do that every age
That existed before their enlightened

Presence is unworthy of memory
While I rejoice in watching the classic
"Casablanca" starring Humphrey Bogart
And Ingrid Bergman depicting a love

Frustrated and foregone amid the turns
Of a world war when America and
The Allies were confronting the Nazi
Menace that was a genuine threat to

Civilization during the days when
We could be proud to be American.

Listening to
Roger Ebert's expert
commentary brought
the artistry and times
to life.

On a solitary Sunday I was happy
To watch a documentary on a
Spicy slice of Americana that
Some today would label the "toxic

Masculinity" of professional
Wrestling in which the enormously
Musclebound wresters bellow and toss
Each other about which isn't my cup

Of tea but my learning of the life
Of the seven-foot-four — five-hundred pound —
World-famous but mostly misunderstood
Andre the Giant was poignant as he

Was always traveling and forgoing a
Family life and was in constant pain.

He died at forty-six
and celebrity came
with a price but he
did what he thought
God intended.

In imitation of the guardians
At the gates before Buddhist temples in
Japan my half-Japanese daughter sewed
Together with herringbone fabric two

Foxes posed in suitably contrasting
Sitting postures with demonic red eyes
Which my ex-wife and I — my daughter and
Her husband — and their Chinese friend — had the

Happy occasion to view inside of
The entrance to the museum of the
Minneapolis Academy of
Art and Design where my daughter's foxes

Are being honored for their quality —
And I am the proudest guy in the town.

Jocelyn connects
so much of what
I love from the past
going forward.

Yao — my Daughter's friend and fellow artist
From China — is calmly observant as
We are having Japanese cuisine in
A restaurant in Minneapolis

When I learn that she animated a
Colorful and exquisitely drawn book
Featuring my son-in-law Eric who
Is eating with us depicting Eric

As a lovably round cartoon figure
Who has a job answering phone calls from
Distressed people with Eric consoling
Them and as he does over the pages

A blue liquid composing the tears of
Sorrow transfer from callers to Eric.

Eric ends up sloshing
inside with tears of
sorrow — artists are
observant.

The distance in the night is palpable
When a train's horn intones its mournful sound
Over the fields and grasses and the woods
Outside of the city alerting me

To the heavy vibration of a line
Of cars throbbing and throbbing in the dark
And it's difficult to determine the
Direction and the distance of the train —

I only know that someone is driving
Somewhere as I listen for the rumble
Of an engine that's hard to distinguish
In the happenstance moment that I step

Outside of my house on a night when I
Woke and had trouble getting back to sleep.

Perhaps only deer
crows foxes and
coyotes are
listening.

There is a reliable moment in
The morning when my noggin dispenses
With lingering drowsiness and becomes
Alert when I'm finished with my chores and

Enter into the sanctuary of
My little bathroom to shave and shower
And beyond the ritual of using
The razor I don't attend much to my

Image because I've seen it all before
But the moment pops with inspiration
As I get glimpses of insight outside
Of the narrow confines of habits and

I grasp spontaneously light-hearted
Ways of articulating new meaning.

With the softness
of the towel that I wrap
around myself
I dry the water drops
dappling my back.

My lilac bush
and apple trees
are leafing out
gradually amid
rainy days.

—*Tekkan*

www.ingramcontent.com/pod-product-compliance
Lightning Source LLC
Chambersburg PA
CBHW040421100526
44589CB00021B/2783